The Red

By **Leighton Taylor**

Featuring the photographs of

Norbert Wu

BLACKBIRCH PRESS, INC.

WOODBRIDGE, CONNECTICUT

Published by Blackbirch Press, Inc.
260 Amity Road
Woodbridge, CT 06525

©1999 by Blackbirch Press, Inc.
First Edition

e-mail: staff@blackbirch.com
Web site: www.blackbirch.com

Printed in the United States

10 9 8 7 6 5 4 3 2 1

Editor's Note
The photos that appear on pages 19 (top), 40 and 44, show species that are found in the Red Sea, but the photos were taken in a different locale. Because no suitable images of the species could be found in a Red Sea environment, these very similar images were used instead.

Library of Congress Cataloging-in-Publication Data
Taylor, L.R. (Leighton R.)
The Red Sea / by Leighton Taylor : featuring the photographs of Norbert Wu.
     p.   cm. — (Life in the sea)
Includes bibliographical references and index.
    Summary: Examines various aspects of the Red Sea, including its physical features, sea life, and human inhabitants.
    ISBN 1-56711-245-5 (library binding : alk. paper)
    1. Red Sea—Juvenile literature. [1. Red Sea.] I. Wu, Norbert, ill. II. Title.
III. Series: Taylor, L.R. (Leighton R.) Life in the sea.
GC741.T39 1999
551.46'733—dc21
                                         98-18249
                                             CIP
                                             AC

IMAGINE A RED SEA

Imagine a long, narrow sea. It can be red. It can be blue. It can be green. Imagine a deep sea that fills a giant crack between two great chunks of land that are slowly moving apart. Imagine a warm sea, filled with coral reefs and bright fish. It has islands made of jewels. Think of your imaginary sea surrounded by desert sands and dry mountains with camels walking through them. Near its shores are ancient temples.

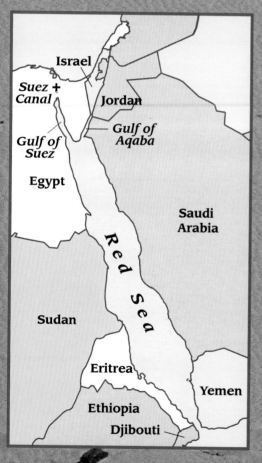

But you do not have to imagine! The Red Sea is such a place! Thousands of years ago, humans began living on its shores and sailing and fishing in its waters. They called their ancient kingdoms Arabia and Abyssinia. Today, the people that live around the Red Sea call their countries Egypt, Sudan, Eritrea, Djibouti, Yemen, and Saudi Arabia. Even Israel and Jordan touch the waters of the Red Sea. They are at the top of the Gulf of Aqaba.

The Red Sea fills a giant crack between the continent of Africa and the Arabian Peninsula. It is very salty and also quite warm. The middle of the Red Sea gets very deep—more than a mile deep. Ancient rocks pushed up from inside the Earth to form islands. Some of the islands in the Sea are formed by volcanoes. Others are made by coral reefs. Usually the water in the Red Sea is blue or green just like most parts of the ocean. But some-times, parts of it look reddish.

That's because tiny red sea plants bloom there abundantly. That's how it got the name, "The Red Sea."

The Red Sea is long and narrow. It is surrounded by land and is an important seaway that connects the Indian Ocean to the Mediterranean Sea. This connection is made through the human-made Suez Canal.

Butterfly fish float gracefully through the warm waters of the Red Sea.
Below: **The Red Sea is surrounded by some of the greatest desert areas on Earth.**

THE NATURE OF THE OCEAN

When astronauts look at Earth from space, they see a planet mostly covered by water. Some people call our Earth "Planet Ocean." That's because it has much more ocean than dry land.

From space, the world's ocean looks the same all over. But it can be very different from place to place. The water can be different. The location and shape of the holes filled by seawater can be special.

How is seawater different from one place to another? Here are three important ways that seawater can change, depending on:

1. how warm or cold it is
2. how much salt it holds
3. how clear or murky it is

Seawater in the Red Sea is very warm and very salty. Very little rain falls there. The sun shines a lot. Water near the surface heats up enough to leave the sea and become part of the air. The salty part of seawater stays behind. Gradually the water gets saltier. Will the Red Sea eventually dry out into a huge pile of salt? No. Less-salty seawater from the Indian Ocean regularly flows in and flushes out the Red Sea.

Very clear water has very little life in it. Water gets murky because it is filled with mud or because it is filled with tiny living plants and animals. Sometimes seawater in the Red Sea is rich with chemicals that tiny plants like to eat. When that happens, the tiny plants bloom and turn the seawater red.

Astronauts took this photo of the Red Sea from space.

7

MORE THAN SEVEN SEAS—THE MANY WATERS OF THE WORLD

The location and shape of a basin filled by seawater gives each body of water special characteristics. The earth's seawater fits into holes of many different sizes and shapes. These giant holes are shaped by the land around them. The names for these different areas of seawater depend on their size and shape.

An *ocean* is the biggest area of seawater. An *ocean* is so big, it touches several continents. It can take many days to cross an ocean, even in a fast boat. The Pacific Ocean is the world's largest ocean. The Atlantic Ocean and the Indian Ocean are very large, too.

A *sea* is smaller than an ocean but still very big. A sea is more enclosed by land than an ocean and may touch only a few countries or even be in the middle of a single country. Sailing the "Seven Seas" is an old sailor's term. In reality, there are many more seas than seven. The Mediterranean Sea is a big, famous sea. It is connected to the Red Sea by the Suez Canal. The Caribbean Sea touches Florida and Mexico and has many islands.

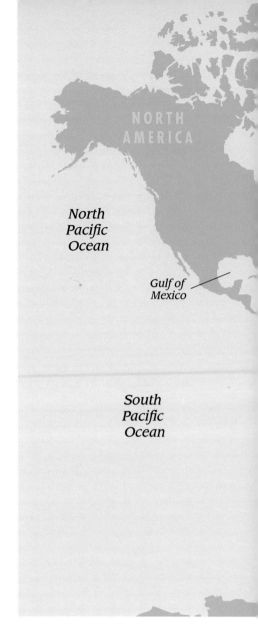

NORTH AMERICA

North Pacific Ocean

Gulf of Mexico

South Pacific Ocean

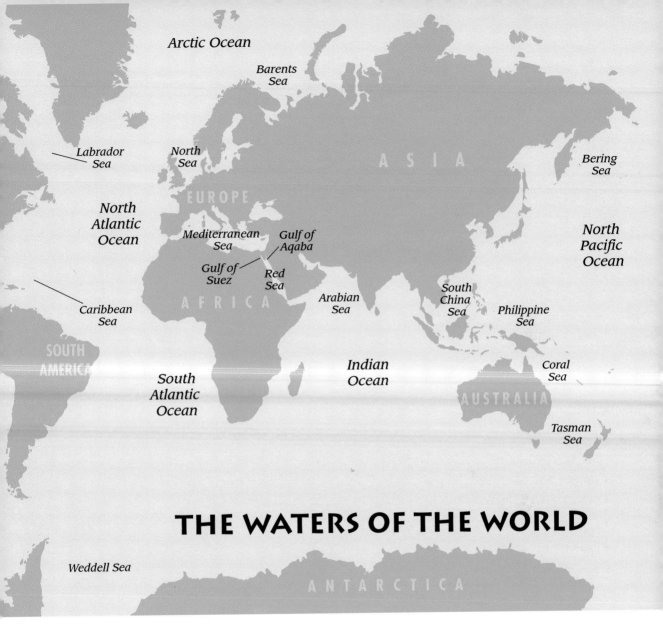

THE WATERS OF THE WORLD

Smaller parts of the ocean can be called a *gulf*. Sometimes gulfs are big, sometimes small. The Gulf of Mexico is very big. The Gulf of Aqaba (AH-ka-ba) and the Gulf of Suez are small. These gulfs are at the very top of the Red Sea.

RED SEA DIVING

People from all over the world travel to the Red Sea to scuba dive and sight-see. The sea is filled with huge coral reefs that swarm with countless species of fish. Egypt is a favorite Red Sea country to visit. Tourists can see the ancient pyramids and then scuba dive in an underwater national park.

Other tourist divers prefer to visit Israel's coastal resorts at Elat on the Gulf of Aqaba. Here, even people who don't like to dive can see the colorful fish and corals on the bottom. They climb into an underwater observatory and go down stairs 30 feet (7 meters) to the bottom.

Wherever they choose to visit, divers can see thousands of kinds of coral reef animals, from large sharks to bushy trees of soft corals to tiny shrimp and crabs. The Red Sea is one of the best places in the world to see coral reefs.

A diver swims through a huge colony of sea fans in the Red Sea.

BEAUTY ON THE BOTTOM, BEAUTY ON THE TOP

Divers in the Red Sea can find animals everywhere—on the bottom, at the surface, and all through the water in between.

Many kinds of coral attach to the bottom. All stony corals are animals. They are tiny rosettes that look like miniature sea anemones with six arms. These soft, round animals live together in a community skeleton they make themselves. That's why they are called *stony* corals.

Their relatives, the soft corals, grow tall and bushy. These colorful colonies of animals look like miniature anemones with eight arms. They don't make strong skeletons. That's why they are called *soft* corals.

Sponges and a few plants grow amid the corals. Shrimps, crabs, worms, and small fish hide in the cracks, caves, and shade made by the corals, rocks, and sponges.

Just above the bottom swarm thousands of tiny fish. When a diver or a hungry fish frightens them, they dart down into coral branches to hide.

Higher up above the bottom swim groups of squid and schools of big fish, such as jacks. Right at the surface, jellyfish drift and turtles come up to breathe.

Colorful fairy basslets hide among the coral. *Inset:* **Large schools of fish, such as jacks, find the coral reef to be a perfect breeding ground.**

RED SEA SPACESHIPS

A streamlined silvery shape speeds forward. It flies out of the bright sky above. Suddenly it stops. A big shiny round eye moves slowly and then stares directly down at an amazed diver below. The diver reaches out. The silvery shape speeds away, propelled by a powerful jet.

Does this sound like a spaceship visiting Earth? It's not— but to many divers in the Red Sea it is something just as interesting. Fast, silvery squid speed all over the Red Sea reefs. Their shiny skins match the bright sky above. Fishes or divers looking up have a hard time seeing them. Curious squid come to divers and look them over carefully with their big eyes.

A squid as long as your two hands has an eye almost as big as a ping-pong ball.

Squids are relatives of octopus, but they have ten legs instead of eight. When it is speeding along, a squid holds its ten arms straight out. When a squid grabs a fish to eat, it uses its strong arms to hold on to its prey.

The squid's "jet-engine" is a long strong tube under its head. The tube pushes out water, which propels the squid in a rush of speed. Octopus have tubes too, but they usually crawl along the ocean bottom.

A school of silvery squid dart across the water's calm surface.

H CLOSE-UPS

ow can fish look so colorful? Different kinds of fish stand out in different ways. Parrotfish have large scales covered with colored skin. Most other fish have many, many tiny cells in their skin that are filled with color. We can't see the cells, but we can see the blend of colors they make [see Discover for Yourself].

Some fish stay the same color all the time. Fish that are good at camouflage can change color quickly. They can control the amount of color each cell shows. For bright colors, they spread the color all through the cell. When they need to be pale, their cells hold the color tightly so not much shows.

Some fish are active and colorful in the daytime. Then, at night, they hide in cracks. While hiding, their color gets dull and dusky. Such dullness helps hide them from fish and eels that hunt at night.

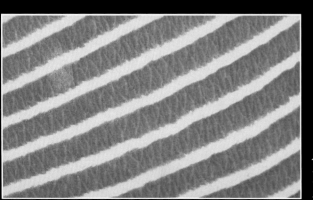

Above: **Close-up of parrot fish tail fin**
Left: **Detail of angel fish**

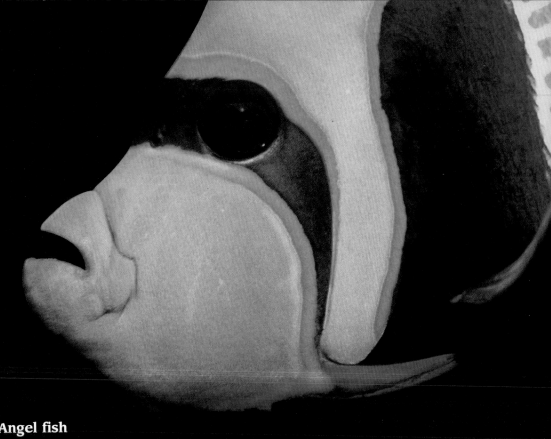

Angel fish

A Fish of a Different Color

DISCOVER FOR YOURSELF

The colors of fish that we see are actually many tiny elements of color blended together. Here's a way to see how many tiny spots of color can blend to make one solid block of color. Use a magnifying glass to look at a color photo in this book. See the many tiny circles of color? Now look at the photo without the magnifier. What do you see? Book printers use tiny spots of colored ink. Fish use tiny cells filled with color.

BREATHING IN THE RED SEA

We humans breathe by sucking air into our lungs. The air, in turn, fills our chests. That's easy to do on land, but divers who visit the reefs of the Red Sea must take air underwater with them in steel tanks.

Stingrays, sharks, and fish, however, don't have lungs. So how do they breathe? Like most animals that live underwater, they breathe with gills instead of lungs. Gills are red, feathery organs inside the slits on the side or bottom of a fish's head. Gills are made of tiny tubes filled with blood, similar to the tubes in human lungs.

Bubbles rise from a diver's tank as he swims past a cave filled with small, silvery minnows.

Most fish and sharks and rays suck water in through their mouths. The water flows over their gills and gets flushed out through the gill slits. Gill slits are the "exhaust pipes" for the gills.

The blue-spotted stingray feeds in the sand. Its mouth is on the bottom of its body, in front of its gill slits. Its wide, flat body covers the sand and stops small shrimp and worms from getting away.

But with a mouth full of sand and shrimp how can a stingray pass clean seawater over its gills? If you look carefully behind a stingray's eye, you'll see a hole. The other eye has a hole behind it, too. Muscles pump clean seawater into these holes. The water flows over the gills and gets flushed out of the gill slits on the bottom of the ray's body. That way, a stingray's mouth can be busy doing other things. A blue-spotted stingray can actually breathe and eat at the same time!

Top: **Large gill slits cover the underside of this giant manta ray.**
Middle: **The blue-spotted stingray uses its mouth on its underside to dig for food.**
Bottom: **Holes behind a stingray's eyes take in fresh seawater.**

19

◀ *Above:* **Moray eels swim by moving side to side, like a snake.**
Opposite: **Morays often hide in reefs with just their heads sticking out.**

EELS IN THE OPEN

Moray eels are excellent hunters on coral reefs. They have a
keen sense of smell and can sniff out fish, shrimp, and crabs that
hide in cracks and caves. Morays usually hide in the reef with just
their heads sticking out. Eels show their long sharp teeth a lot
because they need to breathe through their mouths. The eels look
threatening to divers, even though they are just breathing.

Sometimes eels leave their hiding places to hunt in the reef's open waters. A moray has no fins, so it swims by moving its body like a snake. Morays can swim fast and catch fish by chasing them. It is a real thrill for a diver to see a moray eel swimming across the reef.

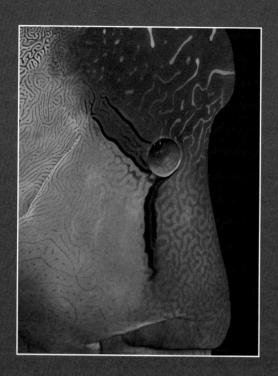

BIG MOUTH AND BUMPY HEAD

Red Sea reefs have thousands and thousands of fish living on them. Most of the reef's fish are smaller than a big man's hand. Some fish are tiny—shorter than your little finger. The biggest animals on the reef are sharks.

The biggest fish on Red Sea reefs is the bumphead wrasse. Bumphead wrasses can be longer than an adult man.

But when it's young, a bumphead wrasse looks very different from an old bumphead wrasse. When it is as small as your hand, it has no bump on its head. As it grows older and bigger, a big bump grows on its forehead. The older the wrasse, the bigger the bump!

And the bigger its mouth. Bumphead wrasses eat fish, sea snails, and sea urchins. Their big mouths can crush shells and spines.

These bump-headed Napoleon wrasses grow to more than 4 feet (1.2 meters) long and are some of the Red Sea's largest fish.
Inset: **Bump-headed Napoleon wrasse**

SEE THE SEA SNAILS

Have you ever seen a garden snail in your yard or in a park? Garden snails are brown and dull-looking. They eat grass and leaves and tiny plants. But garden snails have many beautiful relatives in the Red Sea. They are called sea snails. Some sea snails also eat tiny plants. Others can actually kill and eat fish!

Cowries are sea snails with beautiful shells. Shell collectors will pay a lot of money for a fine cowry shell from the Red Sea. Live cowries cover and hide their shells with their muscles as they crawl around coral reefs.

This cowry is covering its shell with its muscle, called a mantle.

▸ **Cone snails use poison to capture prey. Their venom is powerful enough to be dangerous to humans.**

Cone snails also have beautiful shells. Instead of scraping rocks with a flat tooth like cowries, cone snails spit poison darts. On Red Sea reefs, cone snails hunt worms and small fish that live on the sea bottom. When a cone snail has sneaked up close enough, it shoots out a poison dart. The dart is like a pointed tooth, about the size of a small pin or needle. The dart injects deadly poison into the prey. The darted animal can't move and the cone snail eats it.

SOME SNAILS CRAWL.
SOME SNAILS DANCE.

Not all sea snails have shells. Red Sea reefs are home to many kinds of shell-less snails called nudibranchs. Nudibranchs come in many colors—red, yellow, blue, pink. Some are tiny. Some are as big as your hand. Nudibranchs breathe by using the feathery gills on their backs. Some eat plants. Others eat sponges and corals.

Most nudibranchs crawl along the ocean bottom. But some swim. The easiest kind of nudibranch to see in the Red Sea is called the Spanish Dancer. When a Spanish Dancer swims, its red body flutters like the fancy petticoat of a Flamenco dancer from Spain.

This spider crab—also known as an icicle crab—feeds within the safety of its soft coral home.

STRANGE BEDFELLOWS

Red Sea reefs are crowded with creatures. Many of them can be dangerous. For some creatures, it is hard to find a safe place to live. Animals without a safe place to hide get eaten.

Many kinds of reef animals wait for food to come to them. Corals and sponges eat tiny animals that float by in moving water. Some animals find shelter and food by living both on and in other animals. Corals and sponges commonly host such animals. Many kinds of tiny crabs live in the branches of corals just like a squirrel lives in a tree. When the coral grabs food, the crab shares some of the scraps. When a crab-eating fish swims by, the crab hides in the coral. Biologists call this form of "shared living" mutualism.

An anemone fish finds safety amid the stinging tentacles of its host anemone.

Sea anemones and anemonefish are another good example of mutualism. Like their relatives, the jellyfish, anemones are armed with special poisonous weapons. These weapons are held in tiny cells that cover most of an anemone's body. Each cell holds a dart with a long coiled tail. The darts are bathed in poison. When an animal (or person) touches a jellyfish, anemone, or coral, the cells break open. Thousands of poison darts uncoil and fly out. For a human, the poison darts can cause a painful rash. A small shrimp or fish can die.

But anemonefish live safely inside the maze of an anemone's tentacles. They never get stung. Anemonefish are covered with a special mucus that makes the anemone think the fish is part of it. An anemonefish can hide from bigger fish inside the safety of this special poison "rug." Anemonefish also share food with the anemone.

I SEE YOU!

Fish need good eyesight. They need to find food. They need to see danger and escape. Different fish have different kinds of eyes depending on how they live. Big-mouthed hunters have big eyes to seek out the animals they eat.

Fish that feed at night have sharp vision but don't see colors. Look carefully at the eyes of fish. Different fish have very different shaped pupils in the middle of their eyes. The colors of fish eyes can be very different, too.

Our eyes are in the front of our faces. We can see straight ahead very well. We can move our eyes up and down and side to side but we still see mainly what's in front of us. Most fish have their eyes on the sides of their heads. A fish can move its eyes so it can look backwards and see what's behind it. It can see to the side and to the front. A very alert fish looks backward and forward at the same time!

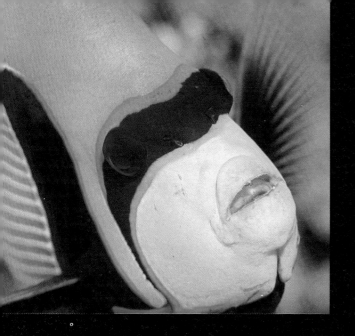

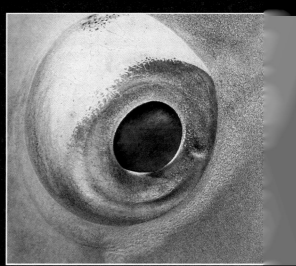

Opposite: Big-mouthed fish like this coral grouper have big eyes for hunting.
Above left: The top-mounted eyes of an emperor angelfish are hidden by its black mask.
Above right: Eye of a sleeping parrotfish
Below: Fairy basslets have large eyes relative to their body size.

🐟 Some fish, like this coral grouper, can change color according to their mood or their surroundings.

BET YOU CAN'T SEE ME!

Some kinds of fish are very good at hiding. Hiding can be a good survival strategy. A hidden fish is less likely to be eaten by a bigger fish. When smaller animals swim by, a hidden fish can leap out and eat them. Fish can hide inside cracks in the reef. But it is hard for a fish to ambush its food from inside a cave. What if it could hide out in the open? If other fish and animals could not see it, they would pass very close to the hidden fish's mouth and then…slurp! The hidden fish has a meal.

Some fish on the Red Sea reefs hide themselves out in the open by using an adaptation called camouflage. Camouflage is the ability to blend in with the surroundings. Fish that have good camouflage include flatfish, crocodile fish, and stonefish. Flatfish and crocodile fish can change the color of their skin to match the ocean bottom. On white sand, they make themselves very pale. On dark sand, they can be very dark. Stonefish can't change color but they let plants grow on their skin. That way, they can hide on plant-covered rocks and be virtually invisible.

Crocodile fish are experts at camouflage. Once hidden, they become nearly invisible in the sand.

BET YOU CAN SEE ME!

Not all fish use their colors to hide. Some fish hide by swimming fast into a crack or hole. When they aren't hiding they stay out in the open. Some fish are so brightly colored, they almost look as if they are advertising themselves!

A school of masked butterflyfish and bannerfish make a colorful commotion in the Red Sea.

Why would a fish want to be so noticed? Some fish need to be seen by other fish. If a male fish is looking for a mate he shows off his flashy colors. That way females can find him. With some kinds of fish, such as wrasses and fairy basslets, males have very different colors from females.

Many fish use bold colors to warn other fish. Bright colors are often seen as warning signals in the natural world.

Other colored fishes change their color and patterns as they grow up. As young fish, they will have patterns that help them match the reef. As they get bigger, their color patterns change. They often become brighter and easier to see.

Inset: **A neon purple stripe near her eye calls attention to this female fairy basslet.**

DON'T TOUCH ME!

Red Sea reef creatures use many ways to avoid being eaten or bothered. Some hide. Some swim fast. Some are deadly poisonous! Poisonous animals are often brightly colored. Bright colors and bold patterns warn other animals by screaming "Don't mess with me!"

Above: **This adult lionfish has large fins that advertise its poisonous spines.**

Some animals have powerful weapons to use if attackers ignore their colorful warnings. Many of these weapons are sharp poisonous spines. Up close they look like needles. Poison is injected when the spines stick into another creature. The lionfish has spines on its fins. Sea urchins have spines all over their bodies. Remember, if you ever dive in the Red Sea, look but don't touch!

This soft coral tree has stinging polyps all along its branches.
Inset top: A close-up of the stinging spines of a fire urchin. Each white bulb is filled with venom.
Inset bottom: A young lionfish like this one has long, feathery fins.

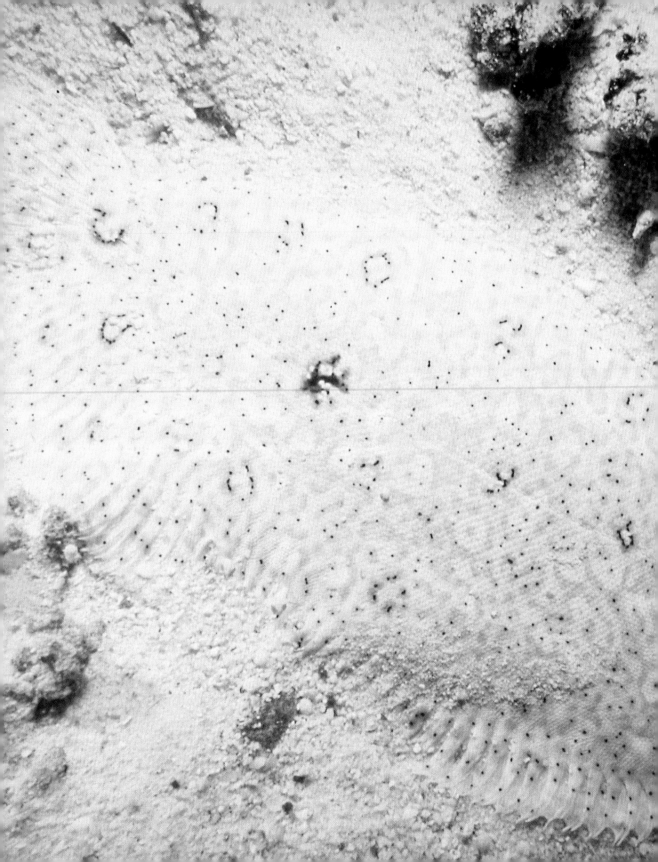

SPIT ME OUT!

Reef animals can protect themselves by tasting awful to anyone that tries to eat them. The Moses sole is a small flatfish that lives in the Red Sea. Soles belong to the same family as halibut and flounders. The Moses sole is named for Moses, the great leader of the Israelites. The Bible and the Torah tell the story of how he helped his people escape death from the Pharaoh's armies by parting the waters of the Red Sea. The Moses sole has a special way to escape death, too.

The Moses sole can ooze a special juice from the base of its fins. This white juice can paralyze the jaws of sharks. When scientists try to feed a live Moses sole to a shark, the shark can't eat it. The shark's jaws freeze open and the sole is spit out! Scientists are looking into whether this juice could be made in the lab and used as a shark repellent for divers.

A Moses sole—camouflaged here in the sand—has a natural shark repellent in its body.

A RELIGIOUS FISH?

Many people like angelfish, but for different reasons. People who keep saltwater aquariums like them because they are boldly colored and exoticly marked. Small ones (about as long as your finger) are colored very differently from adults (about as long or a bit longer than your hand). In a big aquarium you can watch the fish change color as they grow up.

The pretty little angelfish is important to people that live around the Red Sea for another reason. They call it the Koran angelfish. Here's why: Almost everyone living around the Red Sea writes in the Arabic language. But, to people who can't read Arabic letters, the language looks like a bunch of wiggly lines. Sometimes fishermen catch a small angelfish with wiggly lines on the tail that look like they spell Arabic words. The words can look like some in the Koran, the holy book of Islam.

A juvenile Koran angelfish

The Red Sea is surrounded by cultures of the Middle East that practice the religion of Islam. This large mosque in Cairo, Egypt, is typical of many found throughout the Middle East.

The Red Sea's waters wash up along the Sinai Peninsula in Egypt.
Inset: The Sphinx and the pyramids are two of Egypt's ancient wonders.

ANCIENT TEMPLES IN ANCIENT SANDS

People have lived near the Red Sea for thousands of years. The Bible includes many stories that mention the Red Sea. Thousands of years ago, the Egyptians used the Red Sea to travel in boats. Their culture was very advanced. They wrote stories in stone about their adventures on the Red Sea. The Egyptians built the pyramids, the Sphinx, and many other grand monuments.

Arabia is on the other side of the Red Sea from Egypt. There, people built towers to study the stars thousands of years ago. They could find their way across the sea and across the desert by knowing the location of the stars. The Red Sea may have been one of the first bodies of water that humans ever used for travel and study.

Dry desert sands and intense heat make up much of the environment that surrounds the Red Sea.

RED SEA SHARKS

≈≈≈≈≈≈≈≈≈≈≈≈≈≈≈≈≈≈≈≈≈≈≈

Whale shark (world's largest fish)

Many kinds of sharks live in the Red Sea. Some are very large. A tiger shark can be as long as a small car. Whales sharks are longer than a bus. Some sharks in the Red Sea are small. Reef whitetip sharks may be the same size as a 10-year-old human. In just one place in the Red Sea divers saw a whale shark, hammerhead sharks, gray sharks, nurse sharks, reef whitetip sharks, reef blacktip sharks, and also large manta rays. It is a special event when this many kinds of sharks are in one place.

But there is a problem. Careless fishermen are catching too many sharks to sell in the market. More and more sharks are being killed. Divers who like sharks are afraid that soon they will not be able to see any sharks in the Red Sea.

Whitetip reef shark

APPENDIX A:
HOW DO YOU MAP AN OCEAN?

A taxi driver can find an address by using a map and street signs. But how can a sailor find a location on the broad, empty ocean? When a boat sails near land, sailors can recognize landmarks. A map, or even a drawing of mountains and cliffs and beaches, can help them find their way. Some of the first maps made by sailors were made on the Red Sea. We know that the Egyptian Queen Hatshepsut sailed the length of the Red Sea about 2,500 years ago.

But in the open sea, away from land, there aren't any signs. And how can you make a map of a place that is all ocean?

Here's how: All mapmakers have agreed on two kinds of imaginary lines that cover the earth. One set of lines go from the top of the earth—at the North Pole—to the bottom of the earth—at the South Pole. These are the lines of "longitude" (lonj-EH-tood). The other lines go around the earth from east to west. These are the lines of "latitude" (lat-EH-tood). The latitude line that goes around the fattest part of the earth (at its middle) is the called the equator. Above the equator is the Northern half of the earth, also known as the Northern Hemisphere. Below the equator is the Southern part of the earth. That's the Southern Hemisphere.

The equator is easy to find on a globe. But mapmakers also divide the earth in half going north to south. This line divides the world into two halves, too—the western half and the eastern half. Every line is numbered with degrees as they move around the circular earth.

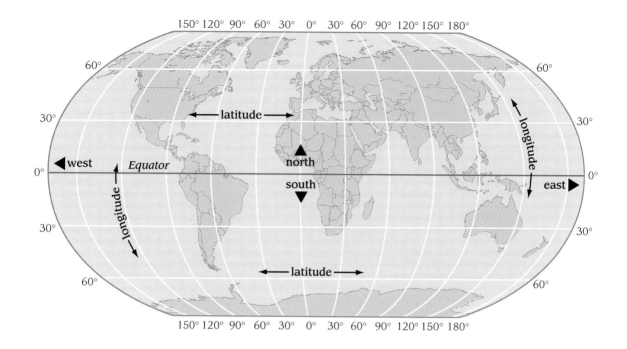

You can find the Red Sea on a map of the world by using "positions." A position is the place where a particular place on the latitude and a particular place on the longitude meet.

Find the longitude line for 40 degrees east. Find the latitude line for 20 degrees north. The two lines will cross in the Red Sea.

But such lines only appear on maps. Nobody can actually draw them on the ocean! So how do sailors find their positions? By looking at the sky! At any given time, the moon, stars, and the sun are in predictable places. If a navigator knows what time it is and can measure the location of the sun, moon, or a few stars, he or she can find a position on Earth.

A new and even easier way has recently been invented. Navigators can use small computers that use satellites instead of stars to find a position of latitude and longitude.

GLOSSARY

adaptation A special way to survive that an animal inherits from its ancestors.

camouflage To hide by looking like what's around you.

current A small or large body of water that is moving slower or faster than the water around it.

density How heavy or light an object is for its size.

Equator The imaginary line of latitude that goes around the waist of the Earth (from east to west).

gills Feathery, blood-filled structures that sea animals use to breathe.

gulf A large part of an ocean or sea that reaches into the land.

latitude Imaginary lines that go around the earth from east to west (side to side). Map makers draw them on maps to show where places are located.

longitude Imaginary lines that go around the earth from north to south (up to down). Map makers draw them on maps to show where places are located.

mutualism Shared living; when two or more animals or plants help each other to survive.

navigation Finding where you are (your **position**) by using mathematics, time, stars, and maps.

oceanographer A scientist who studies the ocean and seas—including their currents, waves, plants and animals.

position The exact place where someone or something is, described as a point where a specific latitude and specific longitude meet.

salinity The amount of chemicals dissolved in seawater. The salinity of pure water is zero; the salinity of seawater is more than 3%.

FURTHER READING

Bramwell, Martyn. *The Oceans* (Earth Science Library). Danbury, CT: Franklin Watts, Inc., 1994.

Clarke, Penny. *Beneath the Oceans* (Worldwise series). Danbury, CT: Franklin Watts, Inc., 1997.

Savage, Stephen. *Animals of the Oceans* (Animals by Habitat series). Chatham, NJ: Raintree/Steck-Vaughn, 1997.

Tesar, Jenny. *What On Earth is a Nudibranch?* (What On Earth? series). Woodbridge, CT: Blackbirch Press, 1995.

Waterlow, Julia. *The Red Sea and the Arabian Gulf* (Seas and Oceans series). Chatham, NJ: Raintree/Steck-Vaughn, 1997.

INDEX